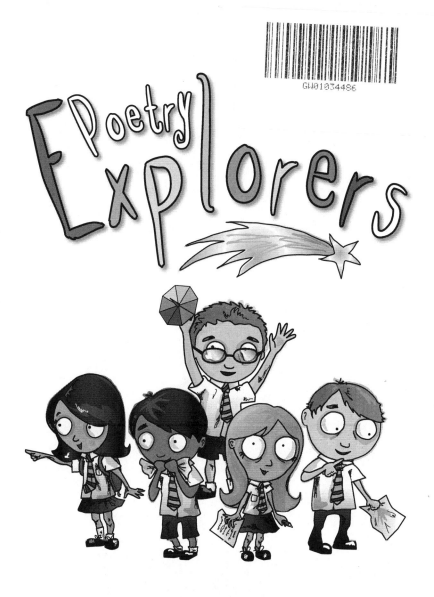

Poetry Explorers

Poems From Northern Ireland

Edited by Donna Samworth

First published in Great Britain in 2009 by

 Young**Writers**

Remus House
Coltsfoot Drive
Peterborough
PE2 9JX
Telephone: 01733 890066
Website: www.youngwriters.co.uk

Foreword

At Young Writers our defining aim is to promote an enjoyment of reading and writing amongst children and young adults. By giving aspiring poets the opportunity to see their work in print, their love of the written word as well as confidence in their own abilities has the chance to blossom.

Our latest competition Poetry Explorers was designed to introduce primary school children to the wonders of creative expression. They were given free reign to write on any theme and in any style, thus encouraging them to use and explore a variety of different poetic forms.

We are proud to present the resulting collection of regional anthologies which are an excellent showcase of young writing talent. With such a diverse range of entries received, the selection process was difficult yet very rewarding. From comical rhymes to poignant verses, there is plenty to entertain and inspire within these pages. We hope you agree that this collection bursting with imagination is one to treasure.

Contents

Kilmoyle Primary School, Ballymoney

St Oliver Plunkett's Primary School, Ballyhegan

Windmill Integrated Primary School, Dungannon

The Poems

Who Is It?

'Go to sleep,' my brother says to me.
I can't, I can't, it's hard to sleep.
It's Christmas Eve and Santa's coming.
What's that? I heard someone humming.'
'It's Santa!' says Tim. 'Close your eyes.'
The door opens, I am surprised.
A jolly old fellow, walks through the door,
He sets out some presents, then some more.
His beard is white, his eyes are blue
And he has a fat belly too.
He eats our biscuits and some tea,
Then he says, 'It's time to leave.'
I see the reindeer outside,
Then Santa gets on for a ride.
He goes to the house next door,
He has presents galore.
We see no more of him this night,
Though everything is alright.
I've got a clip for my hair
And Tim's got a teddy bear!

Becky Stewart (10)
Ballywalter Primary School, Ballywalter

Space – Haiku

Endless sky of blue
Millions of stars and rocks
Meteor showers.

Ben Forrest (11)
Ballywalter Primary School, Ballywalter

My Grandad

Tea sipper
Coffee sipper

Sweet tooth
Grey hair

Embroidery professional
TV expert

Window looker
Money giver

Old man
Slow runner

There is
Nothing better
Than my
Best ever
Grandad.

Lydia Freeman (11)
Ballywalter Primary School, Ballywalter

Jungle

Jungle
Dark, spooky
Exploring, vines, monkeys
All very fearsome animals
Running all over
Nearly there
Out.

Lauren McBride (11)
Ballywalter Primary School, Ballywalter

Cars

Street racers
Glowing neon
Massive engine
Cool suspension
Super brakes
Amazing speed
Loud screeching
Amazing drifting
Noisy exhaust
Green-tinted windows
Coloured bodywork
Police magnet
Coloured rims
Painted body
16-inch wheels
Comfortable seats
What a beauty.

Warren Stewart (11)
Ballywalter Primary School, Ballywalter

Bat

Night hunter
Day sleeper

Wing flapper
Wind runner

Midnight crier
Person scarer.

Laurance Lemon (11)
Ballywalter Primary School, Ballywalter

Cars

Animal killer
Road rage
Sunday drivers
Subaru
Street racer
Exhaust pipe
Sporty body kit
Tinted windows
Police magnet
Cool spoiler
Sporty alloys
Chequered flag
18-inch wheels
Championship winner
Nitro drifter.

Nathan Tyrrell (11)
Ballywalter Primary School, Ballywalter

Waterfall

W here everyday life occurs
A nimals' luxury drinking home
T rout swim free
E verlasting stream
R aining river
F alling gracefully
A mazing view
L ively splasher
L ingering faller.

Robbie Birch (10)
Ballywalter Primary School, Ballywalter

Fireworks

Blue blaze
People gaze

Red shot
Really hot

Purple flies
Baby cries

Orange crashes
Bright flashes

Green spark
Cars park

People smirk
At fireworks.

Dannielle Brown (11)
Ballywalter Primary School, Ballywalter

My Hamster

Cage biter
Finger fighter
Hole digger
Getting bigger
Nest maker
Great escaper
Good faker
Nut taker
Her name is Milly
Very silly.

Emily Chesney (11)
Ballywalter Primary School, Ballywalter

My Gran

Just sitting
Quietly knitting

Grey hair
Patterned wear

Cat keeper
Quiet seeker

Window looker
Money giver

Nothing is
Better than

My lovely
Old gran.

Emma Brown (11)
Ballywalter Primary School, Ballywalter

Once There Was A Monkey

Once there was a monkey
That talked like a donkey
He laughed so much
And lived in a hutch

His hair was brown
And had a crown
He looked so fat
And ate a cat.

Kezia Ward (11)
Ballywalter Primary School, Ballywalter

?

Long tails
Short nails

Some short
Loves sport

Some big
Like a pig

Some fat
Like a cat

Runs wild
Like a child

It's not a frog
It's a *dog!*

Curtis Hastings (11)
Ballywalter Primary School, Ballywalter

My Dad

My dad's the best
He's so cool
Though sometimes he can be a bit of a fool
He's better than the rest

My dad's so funny
He's stylish and football mad
And when he's feeling down, it makes me sad
When he sees me he says, 'Oh look, it's my little honey.'

Victoria Gaw (11)
Ballywalter Primary School, Ballywalter

Fuzzy Feline

Sleepy walker
Night stalker
Water hater
Mouse chaser
Milk drinker
Free thinker
Bushy tailer
Loud wailer
Garden poacher
Dog tracker
Fat pawer
Mouse gnawer
Horizontal eyer
Big surpriser!

Ben Junk (11)
Ballywalter Primary School, Ballywalter

Cousins

C ute, their wee smile
O ut of the house, it's great
U s, we get along when not fighting
S houting aloud, 'Shut up!'
I n the house not good at all
N utters we really are
S ome are really good, some are really bad
   But we really love them, don't we?

Jordan Burch (11)
Ballywalter Primary School, Ballywalter

Rabbits

Hay muncher
Carrot cruncher

Poo eater
Fur cleaner

High jumper
Fun dasher

Good digger
Toy player

Quiet creeper
Soft sleeper.

I am a rabbit.

Ellie McFarland (10)
Ballywalter Primary School, Ballywalter

Mrs Palmer

Mad woman
Gentle talker

Great dresser
Keen person

Kind-hearted nutter
Computer whizz

Problem solver
Code breaker

There is nothing better than to have a friend like her.

Rachael Elmes (11)
Ballywalter Primary School, Ballywalter

Dogs

Ball bouncer
Child chaser

Lead racer
Noisy eater

Bone chewer
Kennel sleeper

Fast swimmer
Food crusher

High jumper
Panting louder

I am a . . . *dog!*

Amy Strain (11)
Ballywalter Primary School, Ballywalter

Footballer

Fast dribbler
Super tackler
Black booter
Gold shiner
Slippy slider
Bad saver
Best scorer
Match winner.

Thomas Darragh (10)
Ballywalter Primary School, Ballywalter

Pearl And Cuddles

Once there was a teddy bear
And his name was Cuddles.
All he wanted was someone to care
About him and his troubles.

There was also a girl
Who wanted a teddy
The girl's name was Pearl
And she hoped her teddy would soon be ready.

When Pearl got her bear
She really was glad
Cuddles also got care
So no one ended up sad.

Rebecca Lemon (11)
Ballywalter Primary School, Ballywalter

There Once Was A Great Big Dog

There once was a great big dog
Who went out and got lost in the fog
He got swept down a stream
Thought he was in a dream
And had to come home on a log.

Richard Kennedy (11)
Ballywalter Primary School, Ballywalter

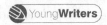

Holidays

Suitcase packer
Plane filler
Sea swimmer
Sunbather
Fancy food eater
Early riser
Beach walker
Show watcher
Apartment stayer
Upset leaver
Hello, now goodbye sun, sea and sand
Holidays!

Abbie Crawford (10)
Ballywalter Primary School, Ballywalter

Me

Evil planner
Metal lover

Gaming master
Guitar player

Computer hogger
Food stuffer

Hair fluffer
Stone flinger

Bad singer
Me!

Jack Chesney (10)
Ballywalter Primary School, Ballywalter

?

Cut tree
Shopping spree

Starts long
It's strong

Gets smaller
Not taller

Write more
To the core

No more
It's only a pencil!

Daniel Gherardi (11)
Ballywalter Primary School, Ballywalter

The Sea

Wave thrower
Light reflector

White horses
Multicoloured

Monster holder
Boat bringer

Body floater
Weed swayer

Rocky cracks
Fish heaven.

Callum Nelson (11)
Ballywalter Primary School, Ballywalter

Wolves

A great howl
A winter coat

A scary hunter
A fast runner

A bushy coat
A fluffy tail

A weird dog
A greedy eater

A bad fighter
A teddy bear.

Jenna Cupples (11)
Ballywalter Primary School, Ballywalter

My Little Sister

Wee squealer
TV hogger
Make-up messer
Toy player
Fussy eater
Good hugger
Fun lover
Fab friend
Attention seeker

Who is it?
My fab sister, Mollie!

Sian Hughes-McKane (11)
Ballywalter Primary School, Ballywalter

The Old Man Of Kilkenny

The old man of Kilkenny
Couldn't stop stealing pennies
He got my five pence
And fell off my fence
That was the end of the old man of Kilkenny.

Matthew Buchanan (10)
Ballywalter Primary School, Ballywalter

There Was A Wee Man From The Dee

There was a wee man from the Dee
Who got stung by a big bumblebee
His head swelled so big
It wouldn't fit his wig
And now to the hills he must flee.

James Kennedy (11)
Ballywalter Primary School, Ballywalter

The Jungle – Cinquain

Jungle
Scary noises
Unwanted animals
I will never be back again
Help me!

Abbi Lawther (10)
Ballywalter Primary School, Ballywalter

The Jungle – Cinquain

Jungle
Lovely noises
Really fierce animals
They jump around most of the time
The wild.

Robson Partridge (11)
Ballywalter Primary School, Ballywalter

Christmas Morning – Cinquain

Oh yes
The time has come
Let's open our presents
Excitement running through my veins
Christmas!

Jack McFarland (10)
Ballywalter Primary School, Ballywalter

Dreams

A dream, a dream
Commonly seen
Unlike midnight TV.
Only prettier
Pretty, so pretty
Creeps up silently
And gives you a pleasant
Surprise in your sleep.
In a dream you never know
Who you may meet.
A dream, a dream
All I want
And more
I can't help but adore.
My dream, my dream
So pleasant you see
A video when you snore
Yet not always nice
Just once or twice
A nightmare
Comes knocking
On your door.

Elizabeth Blackwood (11)

Cortamlet Primary School, Newtownhamilton

Brilliant Brandy

Brandy is cute
Brandy is sweet
Polos are his favourite treat
He loves to jump, canter too
But sometimes he's cheeky, it's true!

He is brown
He never lets me down
He is always eager
Never looking to be leader
He loves to be with his friends
His tail always has tangles at the ends
Oh no! More work for me.

Brandy, he is fluffy
And when you tighten his girth his tummy goes puffy
He constantly gives his all
Even though he's small
But he's smart and I love him with all my heart.

Caroline McBride (11)
Cortamlet Primary School, Newtownhamilton

Dogs!

Dogs are big,
Dogs are small,
It does not matter,
I love them all!

They may be thin,
They may be fat,
I saw one with,
A funny hat.

Labradors, poodles,
Yorkshire terriers too,
I like them all,
I hope you do!

Benji, Cadbury,
Max and Archie,
These are all names,
That are perfect to me!

Alex Smyth (10)
Cortamlet Primary School, Newtownhamilton

Springtime

S pring is when the leaves are growing
P eople jumping up and down
R ed and orange leaves go away
I n the spring, leaves turn to green
N ight and day leaves are growing
G reen leaves are growing quick
T umbling are the leaves falling
I n the spring the leaves are green
M errily swinging in the wind
E verybody has fun.

Lisa Henry (10)

Cortamlet Primary School, Newtownhamilton

Friends

F orever friends
R ight-handed, both of us
I ntelligent we are
E verlasting friendship
N ever do we tell
D ouble trouble some would say
S tick together, BFFL (best friends for life).

Bethany Dundas (10)

Cortamlet Primary School, Newtownhamilton

Flying A Kite

Flying a kite, flying a kite,
Is just like being a bird.
I don't like taking part in a race
And coming third.
Sometimes I see all shapes and sizes
In the sky,
And in my imagination,
I wish I could fly.
When I go out I see a big bright sun,
Just like my grandad and I having some fun.
Kites have happy faces
And they are very cool,
They have taught me how to use
And handle tools.

Dillon Wilson (9)
Edwards Primary School, Castlederg

Spring

It's springtime again, my favourite time of year,
When all the birds come back that I love to hear.
I watch closely to see the flowers grow,
People in the garden using their hoes.
In spring I like to look at new life,
Calves, lambs, bunnies, foals, sometimes find it strife.
Flowers blooming all around,
Sprouting from the ground.

Gareth Hamilton (9)
Edwards Primary School, Castlederg

The Sun

Oh, how I love the sun,
To play in it is such fun.
The shining beams are very bright,
How it fills me with delight!
In springtime the sun starts to reappear,
In winter there is no cheer!
Oh, how I love the sun,
I always knew it was such fun!

Jayne Young (8)

Edwards Primary School, Castlederg

Baby Lambs

Springtime, springtime is the best,
It puts my knowledge to the test.
New lambs are born every day,
I have to feed them lots of hay.
When the lambs are born, I see lots of blood,
At night they lie chewing their cud.
I love to feed the baby lambs milk,
They are so soft, just like silk.

Emma Keatley (9)

Edwards Primary School, Castlederg

Springtime

Springtime has sprung,
It is so fun!
In springtime I love to play in the sun
With my brother and my mum.
The flowers spring up!
Sitting in the sun with my pup.
Every day playing outside, enjoying the springtime.
Breezy sometimes, but it's not a crime.

Codi-Lea Folliard (8)

Edwards Primary School, Castlederg

Spring Birds

The birds come back and make us cheerful,
The birds are rested and not so fearful.
We see all kinds of birds around,
We see them up high and on the ground.
Birds have chicks, they are so soft,
Waddling, cheeping, all aloft.
Feeding them with lots of meal,
My little friend and I, the deal has been sealed.

Jacob Kerrigan (8)

Edwards Primary School, Castlederg

The Sun

I love to see the sun,
When I see it, I have such fun.
It makes the day so bright,
The colours of it are so light.
I don't like putting suncream on,
I hope it will soon be gone.
The sun makes me so happy,
It makes my feet tippy tappy.

Kennedy Hill (9)

Edwards Primary School, Castlederg

Spring Flowers

Spring flowers are so colourful,
I never knew they were so wonderful.
Way down low,
Dancing like a rainbow.
They rest quietly on the green grass,
They are my favourite and class.
Spring flowers are very wonderful things,
I watch for them every spring.

Kerri Hunter (8)

Edwards Primary School, Castlederg

Flying A Kite

Red, yellow and purple too,
I look up to the sky and it's really blue.
I struggle to keep it up in the breeze,
You have to keep it away from the trees.
When my kite goes into the tree,
I have to spend time on getting it free.

Scott Montgomery (9)
Edwards Primary School, Castlederg

Spring Flowers

Spring flowers are so bright,
They sometimes grow to an awful height.
They smell nicer than a rabbit hutch,
I like them very much.
Spring flowers are so wonderful,
They are also colourful.

Emma Reid (8)
Edwards Primary School, Castlederg

Wind

When the wind blows,
Skyscrapers wobble, glasses smash.

When the wind blows,
Branches bend, waves crash.

When the wind blows,
Leaves rustle, kites flutter.

When the wind blows,
The wind whistles, dogs mutter.

When the wind blows,
Doors shut, kites dance.

When the wind blows,
Scarves wave, twigs prance.

When the wind blows,
Dustbins echo, trees chatter.

When the wind blows,
Cats hide, windows shatter.

When the wind blows,
Flowers are gone, windmills are damaged.

Harry Russell (10)
Greenisland Primary School, Greenisland

Wind

When the wind blows,
Trees bend, leaves rustle.

When the wind blows,
Washing flaps, smoke drifts.

When the wind blows,
Houses get damaged, paper lifts.

When the wind blows,
Doors slam, gates creak.

When the wind blows,
Ships rock, lids rattle.

When the wind blows,
Water ripples, electricity down.

When the wind blows,
Kites soar, hair moves.

When the wind blows,
Sounds like an owl hooting and flapping.

Andrew Rogers (9)
Greenisland Primary School, Greenisland

Spaceman

Suit on
Helmet under arm
Cheering and applause
Picture taken
No rocket!

Samuel Brolly (11)
Greenisland Primary School, Greenisland

Wind

When the wind blows,
Dogs hide, leaves dance.

When the wind blows,
Signposts wave, branches prance.

When the wind blows,
Hats fly, the wind rattles.

When the wind blows,
Windows slam, dustbins clatter.

When the wind blows,
Flowers break, windmills creak.

When the wind blows,
Scarves cheer, doors go weak.

When the wind blows,
The umbrellas fly, skyscrapers swerve.

When the wind blows,
Seas chase, trees curve.

Jessica Walls (10)
Greenisland Primary School, Greenisland

Pupil

Sitting down
Pencils out
Books out
Ready to learn
No teacher!

Emily Robinson (10)
Greenisland Primary School, Greenisland

Wind

When the wind blows,
Planes crash, papers flutter.

When the wind blows,
Dogs bark, floorboards creak.

When the wind blows,
Doors slam, branches break.

When the wind blows,
Scarves dance, kites fly.

When the wind blows,
Trees fall, seas clatter.

When the wind blows,
Leaves rustle, windows smash.

When the wind blows,
Dustbins rattle, signposts whistle.

When the wind blows,
Outside's cold, inside's warm.

Jack Park (9)

Greenisland Primary School, Greenisland

The Golfer

On the course
Ready to play
Grab my clubs
Tea in the grass
No ball!

Corey Clarke (10)

Greenisland Primary School, Greenisland

Wind

When the wind blows,
Kites soar, flags flap.

When the wind blows,
Waves roar, trees snap.

When the wind blows,
Hats disappear, penguins huddle.

When the wind blows,
Hurricane's near, children cuddle.

When the wind blows,
Scarves flutter, windows smash.

When the wind blows,
Dustbins clatter, cars crash.

When the wind blows,
Chimneys crumble, cats hide.

When the wind blows,
Clouds rumble, I'm inside.

James Wallis (9)
Greenisland Primary School, Greenisland

Sniperman

At the front line
Bombs raining down
Sniper gleaming
Big tin hat
No bullets!

David McClements (10)
Greenisland Primary School, Greenisland

He Shoots

Shoots, scores
The crowd goes wild
He starts to celebrate
They are now showing the replay
Who scored?

He shoots again

He's shot
But it's not a goal
It's out for a corner
He crosses high for the head
Two goals!

He shoots once more

Tackled
A penalty
He is getting ready
The referee blows his whistle
Hat-trick!

Alex Douglas (9)
Greenisland Primary School, Greenisland

The Car

Shiny red
Four exhausts
Tinted windows
In the seat
No key!

Darcy Osborne (11)
Greenisland Primary School, Greenisland

The Wind

When you open your front door,
In comes the wind, more and more.
Whirling past every ear,
It even sounds like someone's cheer!

You step outside, the back door slams,
The wind sounds like a bunch of clams.
When you're walking down the lane,
The wind knocks you over and causes pain.

You lie there without a sound,
While the wind goes round and round,
Whispering bad things in your ear,
That you might not want to hear.

Wind can be lots and lots of fun,
But can hurt you, like a loaded gun.
So next time it's a windy day,
Make sure you're safe before you play!

Emily McMahon (10)
Greenisland Primary School, Greenisland

With A Friend

I can race with a friend
And chase with a friend.

I can play with a friend
And stay with a friend.

I can slide with a friend
And glide with a friend.

Ryan McVicker (9)
Greenisland Primary School, Greenisland

Wind

When the wind blows,
Leaves rustle, seas roar.

When the wind blows,
Doors slam, smoke drifts.

When the wind blows,
Branches fall, dogs bark.

When the wind blows,
Trees fall, litter flies.

When the wind blows,
Ships crash, knees shiver.

When the wind blows,
Coats flutter, scarves flap.

When the wind blows,
Windows shatter, bins clatter.

Cameron Slinger (9)
Greenisland Primary School, Greenisland

In Our Playground

In the playground
Some skip around
Playing games
Chasing people around
Some want to be famous
Like football stars
Some go lazy and some go crazy.

Adam White (8)
Greenisland Primary School, Greenisland

Cold And Windy

It's a cold and windy morning
Everybody's snoring
But suddenly it starts to blow
All the kids yell, 'It's time to go'
On a cold and windy morning.

It's a cold and windy day
Let's go out and play
We'll fly our kites
And fight the mice
On a cold and windy day.

It's a cold and windy night
The dogs might bite
So be aware
You might get scared
On a cold and windy night.

Emma Harkens (10)
Greenisland Primary School, Greenisland

Wind

When the wind blows
Leaves fall, trees blow.
When the wind blows
Windows crackle, doors close.
When the wind blows
Branches break, windmills go.
When the wind blows
Shed doors slam and it might snow.

Nikita Grainger (9)
Greenisland Primary School, Greenisland

Wind

When the wind blows,
Leaves rustle, signposts rattle.

When the wind blows,
Branches creak, waves sneak.

When the wind blows,
Kites fly, dustbins lie.

When the wind blows,
Dogs hide, hats do fly.

When the wind blows,
Skyscrapers sway, windmills play.

When the wind blows,
Some people lie in bed, but others run instead.

Jack Jordan (9)
Greenisland Primary School, Greenisland

Lamborghini Gallardo

A red, racing machine,
A two-door slider,
A four-wheeled driver,
An aerodynamic window,
A space-wasting engine,
A tight-squeezed boot,
A quad of exhausts,
An ear-bursting engine roar,
A pleasing, compact motor,
A car I hope to get.

Ryan Caulfield (11)
Greenisland Primary School, Greenisland

The Wind

When the wind blows
Wolves howl, doors bang

When the wind blows
Cars crash, dustbins clang

When the wind blows
Leaves fly, flowers die

When the wind blows
Umbrellas break, hats fly

When the wind blows
Waves slam, windows break

When the wind blows
Dogs rush, people shake.

Samuel Courtney (9)
Greenisland Primary School, Greenisland

A Fox

A sneaky creature,
A quiet hider from people,
A secret hiding den,
A farmer's worst enemy,
An animal killer,
A hungry pest-eater,
A mouse eater,
A cunning, furry fox,
A big, bushy tail,
A silky, furry coat.

George Byers (10)
Greenisland Primary School, Greenisland

Adverbs — My Day

I wake calmly
I get out of bed slowly
I eat my breakfast quickly
I go to school safely
I work quietly
I listen carefully
I play loudly
I speak softly
I go home happily
I watch television noisily
I wash easily
I go to bed tiredly
I sleep sweetly and
I dream silently.

Chelsie Guiller (9)
Greenisland Primary School, Greenisland

Sound

I like the sound of cats purring
Lions roaring
Birds chirping
Popcorn popping
Cola fizzing
Children shouting
Teacher speaking
Chalk scratching
Pencils writing
I like these sounds.

Grace Carson (9)
Greenisland Primary School, Greenisland

Lion

An enormous, carnivorous cat,
A blaze of fiery fur,
A thick, shaggy mane,
A pair of bright eyes,
A twitching, black nose,
A razor-sharp claw,
A slowly swishing tail,
A frightening, mighty roar,
A set of ferocious, yellow teeth,
A high, elegant pounce on its prey,
A mammal devouring its food,
A very satisfied creature,
An amazing king of the jungle.

Katie Turk (10)
Greenisland Primary School, Greenisland

With A Friend

I can eat with a friend
And meet a friend.

I can sing with a friend
And ring a friend.

I can swim with a friend
And sing a hymn with a friend.

I can care for a friend
And share with a friend.

My friend is the best friend!

Abbigayle Maddison (8)
Greenisland Primary School, Greenisland

Yosemite Summer And Winter

A grey, stony mountain,
An icy, cold spring.
A large, naturally wild park,
A container of wild, untamed animals.
A natural reserve of wildlife,
A beautiful, lovely waterfall,
An extremely cool place.
A big, green tree,
A drab, snowy hill.
A short, white shrub,
A tiny, colourless bush.
An unseen, cobbled path,
A little, lonely snowdrop.

William Simpson (11)
Greenisland Primary School, Greenisland

With A Friend

I can be with a friend
And drink tea with a friend.

I can run with a friend
And eat a bun with a friend.

I can eat meat with a friend
And greet a friend.

I can ring a friend
And sing with a friend.

I love my friend indeed.

Rachel Campbell (9)
Greenisland Primary School, Greenisland

The Wind

When the wind is around
Kites fly many miles away,
Leaves are pulled to the ground
And many a person has been pushed.

The wind is a very strong creature
That powers through the fields,
Like an angry tiger or monster
Chasing after its terrified prey.

The wind will attack anything
That gets too near,
For it fears nothing
And it never sheds a tear.

Andrew Milligan (10)
Greenisland Primary School, Greenisland

With A Friend

I can race with a friend
And chase with a friend.

I can care for a friend
And share with a friend.

I can sing with a friend
And ring a friend.

I can cope with a friend
And have hope with a friend.

A friend is the best to me.

Ben Greenlees (9)
Greenisland Primary School, Greenisland

The Wind

The wind is the weather
That pulls and that tugs,
It snatches flower petals
And uncovers bugs.

A whisper, a screech
Is the sound that it says,
Telling us secrets
In its own little ways!

A familiar child's scream
From a long time before,
It opens and closes
Your back and front door!

Hannah Murphy (10)
Greenisland Primary School, Greenisland

With A Friend

I can race with a friend
And chase with a friend.

I can play with a friend
And stay with a friend.

I can swing with a friend
And ring a friend.

I can care for a friend
And share with a friend.

I couldn't have a better friend.

Jack Arbuthnot (9)
Greenisland Primary School, Greenisland

The Wind

It makes branches fall off the trees
It also rustles many leaves
It helps to fly on high your kite
Even in the hours of night.

It flies around and through your door
Sounding like a scary roar
It smashes up your cups and dishes
And blows away all your wishes.

You almost feel like you are flying
While you see the flowers dying
You feel it on your neck and face
It's the end of the chase!

Katie Kirkpatrick (10)
Greenisland Primary School, Greenisland

With A Friend

I can shout to a friend
And I can play about with a friend.

I can support a friend
And report to a friend.

I can help a friend
And yelp to a friend.

I can have fun with a friend
And have a bun with a friend.

A friend is a friend to me.

Joshua Young (9)
Greenisland Primary School, Greenisland

The Wind

The journey of the wind makes no sound,
While it is passing by the ground.
The wind rushes along the sea,
Howling and screeching as it should be.

Banging doors and rustling leaves,
The wind sounds like a band of thieves.
While it's flying through the air,
The wind likes to rustle people's hair.

The wind is a trickster, that is true,
But it can be deadly too.
If you don't watch out for trees,
One could bring you to your knees!

Patrick Stocker (10)
Greenisland Primary School, Greenisland

Space Shuttle

An iron and steel ship in the sky
A white and black adventurer
A massive, heavy, airtight flier
A NASA-built gravity defier
A fuel-guzzling sightseer
A fire-propelled rocket
A silver, speeding bullet
A supply-packed, metal piece of machinery
A spaceman-filled, bottle-shaped whoosher
A far, strange planet explorer.

Jack Ford (11)
Greenisland Primary School, Greenisland

The Wind

When the wind whispers,
It batters and booms,
When it's no longer,
It's calm in all rooms.

It creeps into places,
It comes creaking through doors,
When it creeps around the house,
Through all the wooden floors.

When the kites fly up,
The children all peer,
Dogs are frightened,
Their faces full of fear.

Molly Long (10)
Greenisland Primary School, Greenisland

Winter Weather

Nipping air, strong winds blowing
Town streets under a blanket of snow
Noses as red as roses, lips as dry as fire
Eyes as runny as rain pouring down a gutter
Hands so numb we can't feel our fingers
Smoke rising from chimneys and fumes from cars
Now and then they skid around
But children not getting out of bed
Because of the freezing air
In winter!

Harry Moore-Jamison (9)
Greenisland Primary School, Greenisland

The Wind

Let the wind blow high,
Let the wind blow low,
It scares the fly,
It breaks the flow.

It blows your hat,
It slams your door,
It scares your cat,
It does some more.

It pulls that guy,
It freezes my toe,
Let the wind blow high,
Let the wind blow low.

Cameron McCartney (10)
Greenisland Primary School, Greenisland

Cat

A furry, fluffy feline.
A bright-eyed night hunter.
A mischievous, menacing mouse catcher.
A terrible, treacherous bird killer.
A lazy, lethargic hearth lover.
A greedy, messy milk lapper.
A purring, playful wool chaser.
A careful, confident tree climber.
A tame, troublesome tom.
A much-loved, much-hated mog.

Hope McCormick (11)
Greenisland Primary School, Greenisland

The Wind

The wind is here and there,
It seems like everywhere.
The wind pulls at your hat
And sometimes it's not fair.

The wind gets up to things
You didn't even know.
It bangs on your window
And it scares you so.

The wind rustles and groans
And creaks all night,
It scares you so much,
You turn on your light.

Neave Lockhart (10)
Greenisland Primary School, Greenisland

Daddy Dearest

A long term hogger of the television.
An empty, finished fridge.
A large snatcher of the duvet.
An excellent, talented chef.
A hole-in-one golfer.
A 'go along with it' player.
A funny, cheery friend.
A wonderful, night-time back scratcher.
A mummy's thoughtful, loving husband.
A caring, exciting, daddy dearest.

Ana Desmond (11)
Greenisland Primary School, Greenisland

Dog

A squeaky, rubber bone hider,
A treasure-finding, excitable digger.
A sock-eating, slipper-chewing, rubbish-licking menace,
A naughty, noisy cat chaser.
A sharp, squeaky, high-pitched yelper,
A deep, gloomy, terrifying growler,
An unhappy, deafening, demanding barker.
A cuddly, cute, carefree, attention-seeker,
A sweet, silly, sensitive buddy,
A nonsensical, dizzy, ditsy animal.
A funny, friendly, fluffy creature,
A bouncy, playful, cheeky best friend.

Mimi Joffroy (11)
Greenisland Primary School, Greenisland

Penguin

A small, cuddly charmer,
A cute, friendly creature,
A black and white tuxedo,
A perfectly smooth diver,
A flightless, feathered surfer,
An exciting, prolific swimmer,
An extreme, hydrodynamic explorer,
A skilful, enduring fisherman,
A graceful, wacky waddler,
A curious, comical observer,
A loving, caring incubator,
A superbly ultimate species.

Caitlin White (10)
Greenisland Primary School, Greenisland

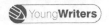

The Wind

The wind whistles a wonderful tune,
Even when you're in the gloom.
It screams and howls all through the night,
In daytime you can fly a kite.
It always seems to be around,
Although it doesn't make a sound.
You always feel it on your face,
It's like you're both having a race.
It makes lids soar into the air,
You feel like pulling out your hair.
You always know that you can hear
When the wind is coming near.

Gemma Martin (10)

Greenisland Primary School, Greenisland

Winter Days

Crispy snow, bare trees
Frosty breeze, knobbly knees
Toasty fire, hands numb
Some hot chocolate with a bun.
Crunchy grass on the lawn
Look out the window, see a swan
Run around, snowball fight
Stare at the sky, nearly night.
Now it's time for bed
I lay down my chilly head
Yes, let's go out again
Tomorrow!

Lucy Millar (9)

Greenisland Primary School, Greenisland

The Wind

When the wind blows
Doors bang, flowers die.
When the wind blows
Windows smash, leaves lie.
When the wind blows
Doors creak, cars crash.
When the wind blows
Dogs howl, people dash.
When the wind blows
Dustbins break, hats fly.
When the wind blows
Waves jump and roll by.

Martin Kerr (10)
Greenisland Primary School, Greenisland

Winter Days

Nipping ice, trees blowing,
All around skies are snowing.
Chapped lips, sore eyes,
Oh, I hate a runny nose!
But I guess that's the way winter goes.
White snow falls so soft and deep,
All night long while children sleep.
Ice on roads,
Shops closed.
Mum calls 'Morning,
Get out of bed!'
'But Mum, I want to rest my head!'

Laura Agnew (9)
Greenisland Primary School, Greenisland

Wind

When the wind blows,
Dogs shriek, doors creak.

When the wind blows,
Waves smash, dustbins crash.

When the wind blows,
Windows shatter, skyscrapers clatter.

When the wind blows,
Umbrellas flap, cats nap.

When the wind blows,
Scarves flutter, winds mutter.

Sophie McCavana (10)
Greenisland Primary School, Greenisland

The Wind

When the wind blows
Doors bang, hats fly.

When the wind blows
Dogs hide, people cry.

When the wind blows
Waves crash, flowers die.

When the wind blows
Dustbins smash, leaves fly by.

When the wind blows
Branches break, I wish it was July!

Matthew McClelland (10)
Greenisland Primary School, Greenisland

My Brother

A tall nine-year-old,
An annoying little menace,
A mad Liverpool supporter,
An untidy younger brother,
A Doctor Who figure collector,
A big burger lover,
An interested, keen footballer,
A spiky-headed hedgehog,
A large imagination,
A very bad loser.

Jordanna Park (11)

Greenisland Primary School, Greenisland

With A Friend

I can run with a friend
I can have fun with a friend.
I can drink with a friend
And think with a friend.
I can read with a friend
And weed with a friend.
I can write with a friend
And fly a kite with a friend.
I would be so sad if there's not one for me.

Lucy Hunter (8)

Greenisland Primary School, Greenisland

Shivering Cold

Biting cold, shivering bodies
Children sledging everywhere
Icy roads, skidding cars
Stepping on crunchy snow
While all around the winds blow
Teens skating on the ice
Icy air makes your hands numb
And your lips go blue
As you slide down the snow.

Rob Devine (9)
Greenisland Primary School, Greenisland

With A Friend

I can race with a friend
And chase with a friend.
I can swing with a friend
And sing with a friend.
I can trade with a friend
And raid with a friend.
I can eat with a friend
And cheat with a friend.
Everyone should have a friend.

James Desmond (9)
Greenisland Primary School, Greenisland

With A Friend

I can race with a friend
And chase with a friend.
I can sing with a friend
And can ring a friend.
I can jump with a friend
And bump with a friend.
I can meet with a friend
And greet with a friend.
A friend is a good person!

Nathan Ramsey (9)
Greenisland Primary School, Greenisland

Sound

I love the sound of a pancake flipping
The sound of a toaster popping
A sea crashing against the shore
Of ice cracking as you step on it
The sound of oil sizzling
And hot water boiling in kettles
I love the sound of leaves
Of a balloon running out of air
These sounds I love.

Lewis Milligan (8)
Greenisland Primary School, Greenisland

With A Friend

I can play with a friend
And spend a day with a friend.
I can ride with a friend
And stay beside a friend.
I can run with a friend
And have fun with a friend.
I can sing with a friend
And ring a friend.
What could be better than a friend?

Jade Rosborough (8)
Greenisland Primary School, Greenisland

With A Friend

I can hike with a friend
And bike with a friend.

I can eat with a friend
And meet with a friend.

I can slide with a friend
And ride with a friend.

William McCann (8)
Greenisland Primary School, Greenisland

Spring

S pring is here, what a beautiful season
P laying outside in wonderful weather
R ain has gone on an April day
I love all the lambs and flowers that grow
N o more snow, days are brighter
G oing out to see the tulips, daffodils and snowdrops.

Laura Struthers (8)

Greenisland Primary School, Greenisland

Spring

S kipping lambs come out to play
P retty bluebells growing big and beautiful
R aining in April, so wet and a bit cold
I n Easter there are chocolate eggs
N ow there is a rainbow in the sky
G oing to see the fluffy lambs.

Leah Spratt (8)

Greenisland Primary School, Greenisland

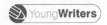
Spring

S kipping lambs come out to play
P retty tulips - red, blue, so beautiful to see
R ainbows shining in the deep blue sky
I n the meadows I see baby birds singing
N o more frost, no more snow, it's all away
G arden leaves and buds start to come back.

Ellen Connolly (7)

Greenisland Primary School, Greenisland

Spring

S kipping lambs come out to play
P retty flowers grow all over the fields
R ainbows shine brightly in the sky
I n the woods fluffy foxes come out to play
N ow the snow has gone
G rass is growing again.

Julliah Allen (8)

Greenisland Primary School, Greenisland

Spring

S heep so soft come out to play
P retty flowers being picked today
R aining water from the sky
I love to see the birds go by
N ests being built with little chicks
G ardens with roses and lily-pinks.

Emma Sloan (8)
Greenisland Primary School, Greenisland

Spring

S nowdrops are starting to grow
P icking daffodils, crocuses and snowdrops
R aining in April, we need umbrellas
I t's my birthday on the 1st of May
N ice woolly lambs and the scent of flowers
G ummy, yummy Easter eggs and hot cross buns.

Heidi Russell (7)
Greenisland Primary School, Greenisland

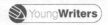
Spring

S kipping lambs playing in the fields
P retty flowers glowing like a colourful rainbow
R aining sometimes, not every day
I love to see the birds flying away
N ests are built with lots of leaves
G oing to the park on a bright spring day.

Taiga Miyamoto (8)
Greenisland Primary School, Greenisland

Spring

S pring is finally here, it will be so sweet
P retty little lambs, always dancing about
R aining sometimes in spring, not every day
I t always makes me think of happy times
N o way it should be foxes eating chicks
G oing to see some spring flowers every day.

Melissa Grant (7)
Greenisland Primary School, Greenisland

Spring

S pring is the time when happy lambs come out to play
P retty flowers grow in all kinds of shapes and sizes
R ain pours down in April
I n the wood there are yellow daffodils
N ests are built by birds and they lay their eggs
G oing out in spring is beautiful and bright.

Richard Byers (8)

Greenisland Primary School, Greenisland

Spring

S pring lambs come out to play
P rimroses are bright yellow
R ain is coming in April
I n the woods animals are wakening
N ests are full of eggs
G reen leaves are starting to grow.

Aaron Anderson (8)

Greenisland Primary School, Greenisland

Spring

S unshine is shining brightly
P lants like tulips and bluebells happy in the sun
R ainbow sitting in the sky after April showers
I n the meadows happy woolly lambs leap
N ow in the fields the lambs are playing
G rowing trees sprouting green leaves.

Tommy Norton (7)

Greenisland Primary School, Greenisland

Spring

S kipping lambs come out to play
P retty flowers smell lovely and fresh
R aining showers in April are coming
I n the meadow, fox cubs play
N octurnal animals come out to play
G oodnight lambs, see you the next day.

Rebecca Savage (7)

Greenisland Primary School, Greenisland

Spring

S kipping lambs come out to play
P rimroses are a lovely bright yellow
R ain is coming in April
I n the trees I see birds building their nests
N ow hedgehogs are coming out of hibernation
G oodnight lambs, see you the next day.

Aaron Semple–Watson (8)
Greenisland Primary School, Greenisland

Spring

S kipping lambs in the field, look over there, I see some
P retty flowers all around us, I love the scent of them
R ain in April, I am getting very wet
I like it when the birds come back and lay their eggs
N ests are being built by birds, what a beautiful sight
G oing home because I'm sleepy, goodnight.

Benjamin Jamieson (8)
Greenisland Primary School, Greenisland

Spring

S kipping, fluffy lambs come out to play
P retty flowers grow all over town
R ainbows are in the bright sky
I n the field rabbits are hopping
N ow the garden is alive with daffodils
G oing out in the sunshine and showers.

Nathan Swann (7)

Greenisland Primary School, Greenisland

Spring

S kipping lambs come out and play
P retty birds are going to lay
R abbits hopping everywhere
I n the long, green grass
N ow the day is over, lambs go to sleep
G oodnight chicks in the nest.

Kelly McClean (7)

Greenisland Primary School, Greenisland

Spring

S kipping lambs everywhere, what a sight
P retty birds are singing in the trees
R ed, blue and yellow flowers
I think it is so lovely, birds building nests
N ow the rain is starting to fall
G rass is growing taller every day.

Jason Magee (8)

Greenisland Primary School, Greenisland

Spring

S kipping lambs come out to play
P laying ball in the sun is such fun
R unning up and down, where did the lamb go?
I love spring when the flowers start to grow
N ow we play in the pool and watch the grass grow
G rowing daffodils and crocuses all day long.

Lucy Jamison (8)

Greenisland Primary School, Greenisland

Spring

S kipping lambs come out to play
P laying all day long, yay
R ainbow-coloured flowers so bright
I love the way it's soon going to be summer
N ests are in every tree
G rowing lambs having such fun.

Zoe Hart (8)

Greenisland Primary School, Greenisland

Spring

S kipping lambs come out to play
P retty flowers in the garden
R ainbow flowers lovely and bright
I love spring because birds build their nests
N ow children come out to play in the sun
G rass is growing because it is spring.

Zach Pattison (8)

Greenisland Primary School, Greenisland

Spring

S uper, it's spring, I love spring, especially April
P lanting seeds with my mom, I just love it
R ain, rain, rain and more rain, that's because it's April showers
I wish that it could be spring forever, but sadly no
N ow spring has lots of cute, furry lambs
G reat, it's still spring, I love to watch the flowers grow.

Nathaniel Ford (7)

Greenisland Primary School, Greenisland

Bird

Ready to land
Into my nest
Food in my beak
All for me
No nest!

Steven Hart (11)

Greenisland Primary School, Greenisland

Snow

S liding down a big hill into a frozen pond
N ow nice hot chocolate and fire
O n the ice, all the time
W inter is a fun time!

Rachel Strange (9)

Greenisland Primary School, Greenisland

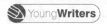
Zookeeper

Bucket ready
Boots on
Ready to go
First day
No animals!

Alison Loney (10)
Greenisland Primary School, Greenisland

Christmas

Going downstairs
Really excited
What will I get?
Open the door
No presents!

Peter Macartney (10)
Greenisland Primary School, Greenisland

Sounds I Love

I love the sound of the morning bell
I love the crickets in the grass
I love the popcorn, *pop, pop, pop*
I love the sound of the water, *splash!*

Justin Stewart (9)
Greenisland Primary School, Greenisland

Wind

When the wind blows,
Vanes spin, hats fly off.

When the wind blows,
Cars crash, scarves flutter.

When the wind blows,
Dogs howl, skyscrapers quake.

When the wind blows,
Houses flattened, caravans crushed.

When the wind blows,
Doors slam, while others creak.

When the wind blows,
Old bones groan, people moan.

Wind can bring death to those who ignore,
So lock up all your windows and doors.

James Gillespie (10)

Greenisland Primary School, Greenisland

Dogs

Dogs so fluffy and cute
Dogs like to go on walks
Dogs like to be petted
Dogs like to be loved
Dogs love to chase cats
Dogs love dog food
And best of all they like to sleep.

Alex Kennedy (10)

Kilmoyle Primary School, Ballymoney

Ten Happy Teachers

(Inspired by 'Ten Little Schoolboys' by A A Milne)

Ten happy teachers went out for some wine,
One fell asleep
And then there were nine.

Nine happy teachers stayed up late,
One overslept
And then there were eight.

Eight happy teachers went to Heaven,
One wanted to stay,
Then there were seven.

Seven happy teachers went to see chicks,
One adopted one
And then there were six.

Six happy teachers went for a dive,
One fell in
And then there were five.

Five happy teachers came for more,
One tripped over,
Then there were four.

Four happy teachers went out for tea,
One went to the toilet
And then there were three.

Three happy teachers went *'Atishoo!'*
One blew away
And then there were two.

Two happy teachers ate a bun,
One wanted another
And then there was one.

One unhappy teacher tried to have fun,
She couldn't be bothered,
So then there were none.

Brandon McKillop (10)
Kilmoyle Primary School, Ballymoney

Five Hungry Tigers

(Inspired by 'Ten Little Schoolboys' by A A Milne)

Five hungry tigers found a boar,
One caught it
And then there were four.

Four hungry tigers climbed a tree,
One found a monkey
And then there were three.

Three hungry tigers found a zoo,
One got eaten
And then there were two.

Two hungry tigers saw a bun,
One ate it and choked
And then there was one.

One hungry tiger stepped on a gun,
He got shot
And then there were none.

Mark Young (11)
Kilmoyle Primary School, Ballymoney

Ten Shiny Bicycles

(Inspired by 'Ten Little Schoolboys' by A A Milne)

Ten shiny bicycles were all feeling fine,
One got sick
And then there were nine.

Nine shiny bicycles were running late,
One was too late
And then there were eight.

Eight shiny bicycles are coming at eleven,
One died
And then there were seven.

Seven shiny bicycles could do tricks,
One fell over
And then there were six.

Six shiny bicycles all went for a drive,
One went the wrong way
And then there were five.

Five shiny bicycles all wanted more,
One had too much
And then there were four.

Four shiny bicycles stuck in a tree,
One fell out
And then there were three.

Three shiny bicycles got some goo,
One fell in it
And then there were two.

Two shiny bicycles had a bun,
One ate it all
And then there was one.

One shiny bicycle had so much fun,
It then fell apart
And then there were none.

Jessica Hodges (10)
Kilmoyle Primary School, Ballymoney

Five Gorgeous Girls

(Inspired by 'Ten Little Schoolboys' by A A Milne)

Five gorgeous girls had to do a chore,
One fainted with boredom
And then there were four.

Four gorgeous girls smiled with glee,
One fell over
And then there were three.

Three gorgeous girls shouted out, 'Boo!'
One got scared
And then that left two.

Two gorgeous girls were having lots of fun,
One didn't join in
And then there was one.

One gorgeous girl found she was having a son,
Went to the hospital
And then there were none.

Tori Hartin (9)
Kilmoyle Primary School, Ballymoney

Ten Cheeky Monkeys

(Inspired by 'Ten Little Schoolboys' by A A Milne)

Ten cheeky monkeys started to whine,
One fell asleep
And then there were nine.

Nine cheeky monkeys started to skate,
One fell over
And then there were eight.

Eight cheeky monkeys turned eleven,
One was only ten
And then there were seven.

Seven cheeky monkeys all ate a Twix,
One was sick
And then there were six.

Six cheeky monkeys went for a dive,
One fell on a rock
And then there were five.

Five cheeky monkeys opened a door,
One broke the handle
And then there were four.

Four cheeky monkeys smiled with glee,
One started to cry
And then there were three.

Three cheeky monkeys wore a shoe,
One was too small
And then there were two.

Two cheeky monkeys lay in the sun,
One frizzled up
And then there was one.

One cheeky monkey ate a bun,
He turned white
And then there was none.

Jessie Gray (10)
Kilmoyle Primary School, Ballymoney

Five Happy Robots

(Inspired by 'Ten Little Schoolboys' by A A Milne)

Five happy robots jumping on the floor,
One jumped through it,
Then there were four.

Four happy robots sitting in a tree,
One fell out
And then there were three.

Three happy robots were turning blue,
One got killed
And then there were two.

Two happy robots eating a bun,
One choked
And then there was one.

One happy robot having some fun,
It blew up
And then there were none.

Timothy Keys (9)
Kilmoyle Primary School, Ballymoney

Sweets

Oh sweets
Oh lovely sweets
Such tasty sweets

Oh chocolate
Oh yummy chocolate
Such milky chocolate

Oh jelly babies
Oh little jelly babies
Such small jelly babies

Oh candy cane
Oh pretty candy cane
Such sweet candy cane

Oh toffee
Oh hard toffee
Such sticky toffee

Oh marshmallows
Oh delicious marshmallows
Such good marshmallows

Oh sweets
My favourite sweets
Such tasty sweets.

Zara Stirling (11)
Kilmoyle Primary School, Ballymoney

Five Happy Schoolgirls

(Inspired by 'Ten Little Schoolboys' by A A Milne)

Five happy schoolgirls mopping up the floor,
One fell over
And then there were four.

Four happy schoolgirls skipping round a tree,
One got bored
And then there were three.

Three happy schoolgirls going to find Sue,
One got lost
And then there were two.

Two happy schoolgirls going for a run,
One got tripped up
And then there was one.

One happy schoolgirl found a gun,
She shot herself
And then there were none!

Abby Jo Johnston (9)
Kilmoyle Primary School, Ballymoney

Five Gloomy Donkeys

(Inspired by 'Ten Little Schoolboys' by A A Milne)

Five gloomy donkeys met a boar,
One befriended it
And then there were four.

Four gloomy donkeys didn't agree,
One went off in a huff
And then there were three.

Three gloomy donkeys yelled out, 'Boo!'
One got frightened
And then there were two.

Two gloomy donkeys searched for a bun,
One didn't share it
And then there was one.

One gloomy donkey, too warm in the sun,
Went into the shed
And then there were none.

Ruth Taggart (11)
Kilmoyle Primary School, Ballymoney

Five Cheeky Monkeys

(Inspired by 'Ten Little Schoolboys' by A A Milne)

Five cheeky monkeys all felt sore,
One went to the vet
And then there were four.

Four cheeky monkeys met a bee,
One got stung
And then there were three.

Three cheeky monkeys went to the zoo,
One trapped himself
And then there were two.

Two cheeky monkeys ate a bun,
One threw up
And then there was one.

One cheeky monkey had some fun,
He played with a gun
And then there were none.

Rachel Taggart (11)
Kilmoyle Primary School, Ballymoney

Five Bouncing Rabbits

(Inspired by 'Ten Little Schoolboys' by A A Milne)

Five bouncing rabbits went through a door,
One banged its head
And then there were four.

Four bouncing rabbits tried to agree,
One did not try
So then there were three.

Three bouncing rabbits went to the loo,
One fell in
And then there were two.

Two bouncing rabbits flew to the sun,
One got crisped
And then there was one.

One bouncing rabbit could find no fun,
He looked and tried
And then there were none!

Emma Creelman (9)
Kilmoyle Primary School, Ballymoney

Five Tough Terminators

(Inspired by 'Ten Little Schoolboys' by A A Milne)

Five tough terminators fixing a floor,
One fell through
And then there were four.

Four tough terminators climbing a tree,
One fell out
And then there were three.

Three tough terminators heard a moo,
One was scared
And then there were two.

Two tough terminators found a creamy bun,
One pied the other
And then there was one.

One tough terminator stole a gun,
Shot himself
And then there were none.

Jack Dowey (10)

Kilmoyle Primary School, Ballymoney

Five Happy Dogs

(Inspired by 'Ten Little Schoolboys' by A A Milne)

Five happy dogs going to the shore,
One tried to swim
And then there were four.

Four happy dogs saw a bee,
One went to follow
And then there were three.

Three happy dogs went to the zoo,
One saw a lion
And then there were two.

Two happy dogs sat in the sun,
One got sunburnt
And then there was one.

One sad dog saw a gun,
It pulled the trigger
And then there were none.

Scott Hickinson (11)

Kilmoyle Primary School, Ballymoney

Winter

Winter's here
The part of year
The children love!

The snow's falling
The ground's white
Yippee!

Snow's everywhere
Outside we go
What fun!

Having snowball fights
Building snowmen
Having a great time!

So in we go
Drinking cocoa by the fire
And falling asleep!

Joel Blair (9)
Kilmoyle Primary School, Ballymoney

Horses

Horses
Nuzzling
Calm and gentle
Patient and silent
Horses

Horses
Galloping
Leaping and neighing
Trotting and turning
Horses

Horses
Pawing
Snorting and rearing
Kicking and bucking
Horses.

Annie McIlhatton (9)
Kilmoyle Primary School, Ballymoney

Cristiano Ronaldo

From a distance I see you, Ronaldo
Running quickly
Fancy footwork
Beating the defender
Stepover, stepover
Scoring a goal
The crowd go wild for him
Man of the match!

Alan Montgomery (11)
Kilmoyle Primary School, Ballymoney

Chocolate

Soft and luscious
Creamy, delicious
Melting in your mouth
Chocolate

Caramel to munch
Nut or crunch
Or even just plain
Chocolate

A little treat
For special days
Makes you feel so good
Chocolate.

Hannah McCurdy (10)
Kilmoyle Primary School, Ballymoney

Me Moving At School

I creep and colour
I read and run
I write, work and walk
I leap and learn
I sing and skip
And frequently I talk.

I colour and call
I stand and share
I count, clean and crawl
I glue and giggle
I draw and dash
And frequently I fall.

Chloe Gardiner (10)

Kilmoyle Primary School, Ballymoney

War

Tank shells
Bullet user
Blood spreader
Men killer
Muddy ground
Metal detectors
Guns fire
Banging bombs
Running, crawling, dying, crying
Bringing tears to people's eyes.

Robert Ferris (10)

Kingsmills Primary School, Whitecross

Tractors

T ractors are working very hard
R ain is falling very heavily
A John Deere tractor is the best
C ome along and have a crack
T he day was cool
O n the day it was exciting
R oaring down the road
S neaking around the field.

Scott Murphy (9)
Kingsmills Primary School, Whitecross

My Sheep

I have one sheep and two lambs,
I feed them every day.
Their breed is a Texel,
They have a dotty face,
Big and fat,
They can run fast too.
I like them too.

Joanne King (9)
Kingsmills Primary School, Whitecross

Fireworks — Haikus

Fireworks are booming,
Children watching bright colours,
Beautiful, sparkly.

Dogs howling loudly,
Young children hiding quickly,
Fireworks are booming.

Deborah King (11)
Kingsmills Primary School, Whitecross

Dog

D oing my homework, I can't wait to see my dog, Flo,
   she's playing outside, waiting for me
O utside, Flo's playing, I'm going outside,
   she's singing, I'm glad
G oing in, I'm sad to go away, I love my dog, Flo
   so much.

Beatrice Graham (9)
Kingsmills Primary School, Whitecross

Holidays

So many places to go,
North, south, east or west?
I don't know,
Where is the best?

Beaches, deserts, jungles and more,
Lots to discover,
There is nothing to bore.
So much to do,
Time has flown and
I will return to see Mother.

Leanne Beavers (11)
Moy Regional Primary School, Moy

My Lamb

Fluffy wool
Skips around
White tail
Grass eater
Milk drinker
Sheep follower
Cute eyes
Four legs
Sleeps a lot
Fast runner.

Nicole Beavers (9)
Moy Regional Primary School, Moy

Dalmatians

Black and white
Dots and spots
Lots and lots
Soft paws
Wide mouths
Big eaters
Collar wearers
Long walkers
Big, friendly dogs.

Hannah Sharpe (10)
Moy Regional Primary School, Moy

My School

M y school is the best
Y ou learn lots every day

S cience is my favourite subject
C ool and fun, we play games
H ide-and-seek, football and more
O pen the doors and go outside
O h, what wonderful fun we have
L isten carefully, the bell might ring, it's time to go home.

Trafford McKenzie (9)
Moy Regional Primary School, Moy

Happiness

H appiness is when I get a new game
A ll of my family share a smile
P laying with my dog makes me glad
I feel good inside when I'm happy
N anny does lots of things to make me cheer
E very day I help her in the house
S he loves to see me come from school
S itting with my family and friends is happiness.

Matthew Loe (8)

Moy Regional Primary School, Moy

Dog

Dog
Loves cuddles
Hyper all day
Take him for long walks
Cooper.

Sasha Lockhart (9)

Mullaghdubh Primary School, Islandmagee

Time Travel

If I could travel time, where would I go? Which year?
If I could travel time, would I be filled with fear?
Maybe I'd go to the Stone Age, but what do I hear?
The biggest ever mammoth!
No thank you, I think I'll just stay here.

Alexander Hawthorne (9)

Mullaghdubh Primary School, Islandmagee

Fish

F ish swimming in the sea
I ce-cold water
S lippery, slimy
H addock and cod are just two.

Sophie Jones (9)

Mullaghdubh Primary School, Islandmagee

My Cat

My cat is such a lazy cat
Although she's skinny, it's true
She eats her dinner from her dish
She eats the dog's too!

Libby Elliott (9)

Mullaghdubh Primary School, Islandmagee

Feelings

Happy, wonderful
Beautiful, sunny, singing
Different today.

Mollie Craig (8)
Mullaghdubh Primary School, Islandmagee

Time To Save Water

Time to save water,
So what can we do?
Don't take a bath,
Showers are for you.

If you use a hose,
It's so much fun,
But a bucket and sponge,
Will get the job done.

Stop wasting water,
Or it will soon run out!
Come on people, stop and think,
We're lucky water is still about.

Conor McCauley (11)
St Columba's Primary School, Strabane

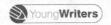

Wasting Water Is Wrong

Wasting water is wrong
Even my mum does it!
Watering her plants and flowers,
I tell her
'Please use rainwater instead
And think of the future ahead.'

Wasting water is wrong
Even my dad does it!
Washing his BMW car
With the same hose.
I plead with him to use his head
And think of the future ahead.

Wasting water is wrong
Even my sister does it!
Taking a bath every night
I beg her to use a shower before bed
And think of the future ahead.

Wasting water is wrong
Even my brother does it!
Leaving the tap running
As he brushes his teeth,
I shout at him that he makes me see red
As I think of the future ahead.

Wasting water is wrong
Even my deaf granny does it!
Boiling too much water in the kettle,
I ask her if she heard what I said
And to think of the future ahead.

Abbie Wright (11)
St Columba's Primary School, Strabane

Saving Water For The Future

Saving water is what I'll do,
I'll not take a bath or use a hose too.
I'm wasting water that's going down the drain,
Why can't I get it into my brain?

In Africa there's a drought
And their water is running out.
Save water, it's the right thing to do,
So I'll open my bin and let rainwater in.

The future doesn't look so bright,
But we must put up a fight
To save water in every way,
As lives depend on our efforts today.

Regan Gallagher (10)
St Columba's Primary School, Strabane

The End Of Winter

On a cold winter's day,
The sea was calm,
The water splashed against the cold, slippery rocks.
It started to rain.
The raindrops dripped into the icy sea,
The waves began rushing to the surface,
As the cold water sparkled
And the bright sun shone on the crystal clear water,
As winter began to fade away.

Bromwyn McGinley-White (11)
St Columba's Primary School, Strabane

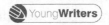

Trickle Bay

It was a beautiful, sunny day
As I walked along the bay
I thought I'd stay and listen
To the trickle of the waters
And the glistening summer sun

The seagulls dived and jived
As the trawler boats arrived
The sound of splashing waters
And the excitement of the catch
Left me feeling rather happy
As I walked along the bay.

Jake Ayton (11)
St Columba's Primary School, Strabane

Our Walk

One summer's day we went for a walk,
We looked up and saw a hawk.
The hawk was brown
And I looked down.
I covered my face
And the hawk took my lace.
I was crying so loud,
There was a big, black cloud.
My mammy came,
When I lost my gem.
She was so cross
With me and my brother, Ross.

Ciara Curran (8)
St Eugene's Primary School, Lisnaskea

Snow, Snow!

In December snow falls all day long
Fluttering, floating gently to the ground.
Outside it is a winter wonderland
Snow is a crunchy carpet.
Heaven sprinkles icing sugar everywhere
The bushes in my garden look like yummy ice cream cones.
The trees go shopping and get fluffy, white coats
It makes my house into a big cake covered in white icing.
Snow is just like glitter from a pretty picture.

Snow, snow, I so love it.
Snow sounds like children giggling and laughing,
Yelling and screaming.
Snow is throwing snowballs
Ice skating, sleighing down my hill.
It is heavenly snow angels
Looking down on Sir Snowman sitting in my snowy garden.
Snow, snow, snow, snow
How I love the snow!

Ailís McGoldrick (11)
St Eugene's Primary School, Lisnaskea

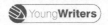

The Jungle

I live in the jungle
In a mighty, old tree
Eating lots of chocolate
And drinking cups of tea

I live in the jungle
In a mighty, old tree
Talking to cheetahs
And feeding birdies

I live in the jungle
In a mighty, old tree
Petting Zebe, my pet parakeet
And swinging from tree to tree

I live in the jungle
In a mighty, old tree
Nobody came to my party
Because they don't like tea.

Aoibhinn McGoldrick (9)
St Eugene's Primary School, Lisnaskea

Dramatic Girl

My dad tells me I have to go to drama,
But I don't want to.
So this is what I do,
I scream and shout and stomp my feet.

When my ma tells me to eat my greens,
This is what I do,
I get my plate and throw it around!
After that I get sent to my room and start to shout!
After my sleep I feed the sheep,
But if they don't come I get angry again.

In the morning I get my bread,
If it's brown I go to town
Screaming for my white bread.
Mum howls and scowls and I go to my room,
Then I'm sent off to school with an empty stomach.

Caoimhe McManus (9)

St Eugene's Primary School, Lisnaskea

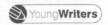

A Magic Medicine

A magic medicine it shall be,
Strong, cold tea from the sea.
A green puppy dog's tail
And a shell of a snail.
A cockroach's head
And a poisonous lead.
Grandma will surely run away,
I am almost ready, so they say.
A bottle of slime
And a bug that can climb.
A singer's messy hair,
A woman's nail whose name is Clare.
I'll make it with a bit of a bone
And finally a wire from a Vodafone.

Marc Hennessy (8)
St Eugene's Primary School, Lisnaskea

The Sea

The sea, the sea is just me.
Then I thought it could be.
So I went fishing and saw people kissing.
I thought, *but it's just not me!*
The sea, the sea is just not me!
I tried again
But it was too much pain.
Although the doctor checked
And he did inject,
The sea is still not me!

Barney McFadden (10)
St Eugene's Primary School, Strabane

What A Year I've Had

In January I saw a cat
And he was very fat.

In February I saw a pig
And he was doing a little jig.

In March I saw a hen
And he was chasing my cousin, Ben.

In April I saw a cow
And she was taking a bow.

In May I saw a sheep
And he was lying in a heap.

In June I saw a snake
And he was baking a cream cake.

In July I saw a bird
And he was saying a bad word.

In August I saw a rat
And he was wearing a baseball hat.

In September I saw a duck
And he was working on the truck.

In October I saw a mouse
And he was eating a louse.

In November I saw a dog
And he was lying on a log.

In December I saw a bear
And he was going to the fair.

Keelin Devine (11)
St Eugene's Primary School, Strabane

Hobbies

On Monday I played skipping
And went down fishing.

On Tuesday I went swimming
And kept on winning.

On Wednesday I played tag
And my sister fell over a bag.

Thursday came and went
Then I camped out in a tent.

Friday it was cool
So I went down to the pool.

When Saturday came
I was fed up with games.

So I stayed at home
And ate an ice cream cone.

Susan McKenna (10)
St Eugene's Primary School, Strabane

Football

My favourite hobby is football.
I went to the match and saw a sight,
Because all the team were wearing tights!

I went to a match,
But the pitch had a patch.
When we got home,
I was covered in foam.

Tiarnán Connolly (10)
St Eugene's Primary School, Strabane

Idea At School

I had an idea at school
It was to take out the swimming pool
My brother and sister gave me a hand
And so we began with my plan.
We filled it with water as the sun shone down
We put on our swimming pants to cool down
Hours of fun on a warm summer's day
The boys and girls in Bearney know how to play.

Rhys McAnenny (9)
St Eugene's Primary School, Strabane

My Poem

My mum is like an ox
Because she is as clever as a fox.
My brother is like a monkey
Because he climbs all day.
My sister is like a lion
Because she roars all day.
My dad is like an orang-utan
Because he is so hairy.

Malachy Coyle (11)
St Eugene's Primary School, Strabane

Family Of Animals

My mum is like a beaver
Because she works all the time
My dad is like a bear
Because he is a great fisher
My sister is like a cat
Because she hits me like a rat
My other sister is like a lion
Because she has a long mane.

Devon West (9)
St Eugene's Primary School, Strabane

Lion At School

I came across a lion on the way to school,
His roar was very loud and his kick was very hard.
I hid him in my bag so that the teacher would not see.
He stayed there very quietly until frightened by my
                                        brother, Malachy.

Karl Coyle (10)
St Eugene's Primary School, Strabane

The Magic Box

(Based on 'Magic Box' by Kit Wright)

I will put in my magic box . . .
Sheep moving fast.
It has knuckles for hinges
And some footballs for a roof.

I will put my magic box under my bed,
Until I wake up without my head.

I will put in my magic box . . .
A window to see Stamford Bridge.

I will put in my magic box . . .
Heavy thunder and lightning in the sky.

You can see all the houses beside my magic box.
I will put in my magic box . . .
The smell of my favourite dinner -
Burgers and chips.

My box is red all over
With a bit of orange -
My favourite colour.

Patrick Burns (8)
St Joseph's Primary School, Crumlin

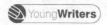

My Mysterious Box

(Based on 'Magic Box' by Kit Wright)

I will put in my box . . .
A friendly lion,
The sound of trumpets playing
And the purple night sky.

I will put in my box . . .
The golden sunshine,
The smell of exotic, yellow daffodils
And also a talking dog.

When I open the door
It will lead to a treasure island with mermaids.
The hinges are made of gold
And the lid is made from leaves.
My box is made of silky pink fabric
And real stars.
I will keep it at the bottom of a treasure chest,
In the ocean.

Emma Watson (8)
St Joseph's Primary School, Crumlin

My Brill Box

(Based on 'Magic Box' by Kit Wright)

I will put in my box . . .
A Chihuahua walking and talking,
The colour of velvet violet,
Two very small people in a village
Jumping up and down.

I will put in my box . . .
A human flying
And a mountain crashing.
Shining sunshine and fresh air.

There is a doorway to immortality
On the top of the precious box.
Its hinges are silver and pink.
Inside is golden and red
With ancient pictures on it.
I'll hide it in my wardrobe.

Abigail Murphy-Donnelly (8)
St Joseph's Primary School, Crumlin

The Bubblegum Box

(Based on 'Magic Box' by Kit Wright)

I will put in my box . . .
A dog running fast
And the church bells ringing.

I will put in my box . . .
Roaring, red people
And the shine of the sun.

I will put in my box . . .
A tree singing and dancing.

The little door in my box
Leads to Disneyland.
The hinges are made out of rubbers.

My box is made from bubblegum.
I will keep my box hidden in my bed,
Under my pillow.

Niamh McCaughley (8)
St Joseph's Primary School, Crumlin

The Magic Box

(Based on 'Magic Box' by Kit Wright)

I will put in my magic box . . .
a football kit.

I will put in my magic box . . .
three cats.

I will put in my magic box . . .
a beautiful taste of chocolate.

I will put in my magic box . . .
thunder and lightning.

I will put in my magic box . . .
speeding in a Ferrari.

I will put in my magic box . . .
my favourite colour blue.

I'll leave my box under the pitch at Stamford Bridge.

Padraig Hanna
St Joseph's Primary School, Crumlin

In My Box

(Based on 'Magic Box' by Kit Wright)

I will put in my box . . .
The sound of music playing.

I will put in my box . . .
A purple elephant slowly walking up a tree.

I will put in my box . . .
The roaring thunder.

I will put in my box . . .
Me eating my roast dinner
Whilst looking at the beautiful Alps.

My box is made of curry.
I'll keep my box inside my bed.

In my box is a secret door,
It leads to the future.

Christopher McGowan (8)
St Joseph's Primary School, Crumlin

My Man United Box

(Based on 'Magic Box' by Kit Wright)

I will put in my box . . .
A bowl of melted chocolate.

I will put in my box . . .
The sound of music playing on my iPod.

I will put in my box . . .
The colour red.

I will put in my box . . .
A swimming pool that I will swim in all day.

I will put in my box . . .
A pancake.

The outside of my box will be red
With Man United badges.

Séan Lagan (7)
St Joseph's Primary School, Crumlin

The Box Of Curry

(Based on 'Magic Box' by Kit Wright)

I will put in my box . . .
A dozen roses that smell like cherries,
Perfume and roses.

I will put in my box . . .
A lifetime of day and night,
The sun and moon together at night.

My box will be made of curry and chips.
My box will be made of love and laughs.

There is a land in my box made of gold,
It is very, very, very cold.

I will put my box under my bed,
Where no one will find it.

Anna Monaghan (8)
St Joseph's Primary School, Crumlin

My Box

(Based on 'Magic Box' by Kit Wright)

I will put in my box . . .
A dog waggling its tail up high in the sky,
A baby getting a soft lullaby sung to it
And a perfect, pink flower that smells sweet.

I will put in my box . . .
Freezing snow,
The delicious smell of a roast dinner cooking
And two snowflakes the same size and shape.

My box has a door that takes me to Candyland,
It is made of flowers and hearts.
I'll keep my box on the top of a cloud.

Beth Hamill (8)

St Joseph's Primary School, Crumlin

My Wacky Box

(Based on 'Magic Box' by Kit Wright)

I will put in my box . . .
Three little puppies and kittens.

I will put in my box . . .
All the girls in the world except the ones I like.

I will put in my box . . .
A swimming pool the size of the world.

I will put in my box . . .
A secret door that takes you to Candyland.

Chris Grant (8)

St Joseph's Primary School, Crumlin

My Box

(Based on 'Magic Box' by Kit Wright)

I will put in my box . . .
A bouncing bunny
And the moon sparkling on the sea.
I will put in my box . . .
A sky of blue,
A bunch of roses and winter snow.
The top of it is made of gold.
I will hide it in my school bag.

Jennie Burns
St Joseph's Primary School, Crumlin

The Magic Box

(Based on 'Magic Box' by Kit Wright)

I will put in my box . . .
A running dog and a songbird.
I will put in my box . . .
A snowy day and a bird.
I will put in my box . . .
A red car in a race.
I will put in my box . . .
100 sweet roses and a pizza.

Rachel Torbitt
St Joseph's Primary School, Crumlin

Animals At Night

Beautiful animals,
Running around,
Playing about through the night.
Jumping, running fast like the wind,
Under the dark night sky,
You can't see them,
But if you get too close,
They run away at the speed of light.
Animals running about all night,
Some might sneak up
And give you a fright.
Lots of animals out at night.

Karen Mellon (9)
St Malachy's Primary School, Glencull

My Favourite Things

The presence of angels, a wonderful thing
Having a bowl of my favourite ice cream
Snuggles and cuddles and soft babies' feet
That fleeting moment my house is tidy and neat.

Sweet memories to cherish, tears of sadness and joy
Pictures in albums, my really cool toy.

The power of prayer, uninterrupted sleep
Making a promise I know I will keep.

Sitting and thinking of my favourite things
Like cupcakes, games and doves' wings.

Shannon Monaghan (11)
St Malachy's Primary School, Glencull

Winter

Today we are on the hills.
Slippery like the Jamaican
Bobsleigh team
The frost is crisp
Like iceberg lettuce.
So we all know we'll hear
'Ho, ho, ho.'
The snow is thick like
The icing on the Christmas cake.
I can't wait to get home
Where it's warm as fresh toast.

Eoin Kelly (11)
St Malachy's Primary School, Glencull

When I'm feeling Happy

Smiling faces
Happy faces
Jolly laugh
Tiny giggle
Big smile
Having fun
So delighted
Feeling great
Fun time
So glad
Excited jump.

Fiona Canavan (9)
St Malachy's Primary School, Glencull

Winter Poem

One night I saw something white,
Flakes falling from the sky.
They lay on the ground
Like a blanket on my bed.
Two snowflakes falling like diamonds.
I lit the fire and made some soup,
All together it was so good.
I went to bed with the blanket over my head.
Like a caterpillar in my cocoon.

Hannah Monaghan (9)
St Malachy's Primary School, Glencull

The Jungle

J ungle monkeys in the trees
U nder the leaves and in the sky
jungle animals walk and fly
N umbers of animals all around
G rass, sun and lovely trees all in the jungle breeze
L ions, tigers, all big cats, get their catch
E lephants at the waterhole and the happy hippos
have a ball!

Laura Owens (10)
St Malachy's Primary School, Glencull

Winter Poem

The sky is as blue as a river.
The snowman is as white as a page.
The snowman shivers like a branch on a windy day.
My feet sink into the snow like I'm walking on a sponge.
My feet are as cold as Jack Frost's fingertips.
I go inside, the fire glows like a moon on a dark night.
I am as warm as a bug in a rug.

Aaron McAnenly (10)
St Malachy's Primary School, Glencull

In The Giant's Fridge

In the giant's fridge
There is a giant ham
But the giant prefers a nice big ram

In the giant's fridge
There is a boiled head
He grinds human bones
To make his bread

In the giant's fridge
There is a crocodile tongue
But the giant's son
Thinks they're lots of fun

In the giant's fridge
There is mice cream
And the pig is supreme
Oh I want to scream!

Connor Chappell (9)
St Martin's Primary School, Garrison

My World

My world has the sweet, succulent taste of a strawberry
It has the scent of a special romantic perfume.

My world has the touch of a soft silky blanket
Decorated with stars and hearts.
My world is my best friend.
Her favourite colours are
Pretty purple and precious pink.

My world's atmosphere is electric.
The people are excited as the tension
And anxiety of the wait prolongs.
They wait to see the imagination
And the creativity of my world.

In my world I can see the beautiful sights
Of New York City
And marvellous sights of Heaven.
The sights of Heaven look like a big fluffy cloud
Floating across the air beautifully.

I love my world.
Why don't you come in too?

Aisling McGurl (11)
St Martin's Primary School, Garrison

In The Giant's Fridge

In the giant's fridge
You'd always think you'd scream
Because when you open the door
You see some gruesome mice cream.

In the giant's fridge
You see some horses' legs
And if you think that's bad
You don't want to see the crocodile's eggs.

In the giant's fridge
You can see some sausage trolls
I wouldn't like them, would you?
Because they look like dead moles.

In the giant's fridge
There is some beetles' mud
And if you want a drink with it
There's always bats' blood!

Rebecca McGorty (10)
St Martin's Primary School, Garrison

The Terrified Owl

Down in the forest at night
An owl got a terrible fright
When out of the dark
Came a terrible bark
And the owl knew things weren't right.

Oisin Doherty (10)
St Martin's Primary School, Garrison

Things I Like To Do

I like playing in the pool,
And diving in is really cool,
Going on bike rides with my dad,
But sometimes things get a little bit mad!

Learning new dances,
Frills and prances,
Eating cold vanilla ice cream,
Then letting out a high-pitched scream.

Playing aeroplanes with my sister, Dearbhla,
And getting wet without my umbrella.
Golfing on my Nintendo Wii,
Then watching the X Factor on TV.

Having fun with my puppy, Sam,
Giving her something to eat, like ham.
These are the things I like to do,
Why don't you join in with me too?

Sinead McGurl (9)
St Martin's Primary School, Garrison

Dog

Postman hater
Cat hater
Bone burier
Cat chaser
Car chaser.

Darragh Treacy (10)
St Martin's Primary School, Garrison

Spring

Spring is coming,
Animals are wakening up.
Flowers are starting to bloom,
Daffodils and buttercup.

Birds are singing in the trees,
And the leaves are swaying in the breeze.
Lambs are jumping, oh so high,
Lots more sun in the sky.

Spring is my favourite season,
And I think you know the reason.
Winter has past,
And spring is here at last!

Michelle Keegan-Rattcliff (11)
St Martin's Primary School, Garrison

Cat

Playful
Affectionate
Adventurous
Cat
Prowling to their prey
Silently
Energetically
As graceful as a swan
I would be lost without you
Cat
Magnificent cats.

Catie Wadsworth (10)
St Martin's Primary School, Garrison

In The Giant's Fridge

In the giant's fridge is sticky sausage foal
In the giant's fridge is a headless troll
In the giant's fridge is a hairy bat
In the giant's fridge is the eyes of a rat.

In the giant's fridge is green goats' legs
In the giant's fridge is freaky frog eggs
In the giant's fridge is a lions' head
In the giant's fridge is a snake that's not dead.

In the giant's fridge is a hamster tail
In the giant's fridge is the shell of a snail
In the giant's fridge is things you can't see
You'll get sick, that's what happened to me!

Aoife Leonard (10)
St Martin's Primary School, Garrison

When My Mummy Makes Me Happy

Mummy makes me happy
Whenever she laughs
Mummy makes me happy
When we're having fun
Mummy makes me happy
When she is around
Mummy makes me happy
When she makes me cakes
Mummy makes me happy
When she sings me a song.

Jordan Daly (10)
St Martin's Primary School, Garrison

Bullying

A is for anti-bullying
N o bullying please
T oo much bullying is not nice
I n a day's work try not to bully.

B ullying is not nice to do to children
U nder their backs don't call them names
L ovely children should not be picked on
L ovely children get rewards for being good
Y our classmates should not be bullied
I n class be very good
N ice in class and all around us
G ood children don't change into bullies.

Cianna Treacy (9)
St Martin's Primary School, Garrison

In The Giant's Fridge

In the giant's fridge
There are horses' legs
And a mix of crocodile eggs.

In the giant's fridge
There is a hairy rat
And a bloody bat.

In the giant's fridge
There is snail stew
I would not eat it, would you?

Katie Stewart (10)
St Martin's Primary School, Garrison

Happiness

Happiness is the colour blue, bright and beautiful.
Happiness is when you know
That all your hard work has paid off.
Happiness is when all your dreams come true.
Happiness is like a pretty, perfect and purple poppy.
Happiness is the scorching and the surprising sun
That is always shining.
Happiness is what everyone wants.

Meghan McTernan (11)
St Martin's Primary School, Garrison

Furious

When I am furious
I feel very mad
When I am furious
I make people sad
When I am furious
I push and pull
When I am furious
I feel mad as a bull.

Conor McGowan (10)
St Martin's Primary School, Garrison

My Dog, Biscuit

On Christmas morning I got out of bed,
Santa had come with a dog that doesn't need to be fed
His fur is light brown and his tail goes round and round.
He barks, shakes and nods his head,
The first night I had him I cuddled him in bed.

Bronagh Treacy (8)
St Martin's Primary School, Garrison

Proud

Proud is when you do a test
Proud is when you do your best
Proud is when you say hooray
When you're happy at the end of the day.

Lorena McIntyre (10)
St Martin's Primary School, Garrison

The Crocodile

Sharp teeth
Long body
Green back
Eats fish
Loves water
Beady eyes.

Eimear McCann (8)
St Oliver Plunkett's Primary School, Ballyhegan

The Elephant

Sharp tusks
Big hooves
Very fat
Can't fly
Land lover
Not fluffy
Very tall
Leaf eater
Warm blood
Wild animal
My favourite
Big ears
At the zoo.

Feithlinn Morgan (9)
St Oliver Plunkett's Primary School, Ballyhegan

A Lion

Good hunter
Sharp teeth
Loves meat
Fast runner
Jumps high
Climbs trees
Short whiskers
Long tail
Big ears
Hates fish.

Conor Fearon (9)
St Oliver Plunkett's Primary School, Ballyhegan

Friendship

F riendship is amazing and causes happiness
R emember friends are there for you
I always remember my friends
E verlasting
N obody will forget friends
D on't fall out
S orry is what we have to say when we fall out
H appiness is what we like
I never forget friendship
P als forever.

Alisha McGowan (9)

St Oliver Plunkett's Primary School, Ballyhegan

Ladybirds

L adybirds can fly high
A nd have shells to protect
D ad ladybird comes to see them
Y ou better watch out
B aby ladybird is so small
I think she is so loving
R ed and black dots they have
D ots and dots and dots
S o small you can hardly see them.

Caitlin Kerr (10)

St Oliver Plunkett's Primary School, Ballyhegan

Koala

Climbs trees
Grey and white fur
Big ears
Big nose
Cuddly animal
Eats leaves
Cannot be a pet

Fionnuala Murray (9)
St Oliver Plunkett's Primary School, Ballyhegan

Matthew

M is for muddy Matthew
A is for happy Anton
T is for Tom
T is for naughty Terry
H is for happy
E is for Emma
W is for window.

Anton O Hagan (7)
St Oliver Plunkett's Primary School, Ballyhegan

Karate

K is for karate Kerry
A is for accident Andy
R is for robber Ryan
A is for actress Andy
T is for twilight Tony
E is for expert Emmer.

Jack Hughes (8)
St Oliver Plunkett's Primary School, Ballyhegan

The Lion

Meat eater
Big mane
Sharp teeth
Good hunter
Furry tail
Good climber.

Matthew Turbitt (7)
St Oliver Plunkett's Primary School, Ballyhegan

Rally

R ally cars are fast
A ll rally cars are different colours
L arry is my dog's name
L arry jumps on you
Y ou need to brush your teeth.

Jamie McKenna (8)
St Oliver Plunkett's Primary School, Ballyhegan

Leah

L is for pretty Leah
E is for beautiful Eimear
A is for cool Anton
H is for happy Hannah.

Leah Moffitt (7)
St Oliver Plunkett's Primary School, Ballyhegan

Rome

R arely a storm occurs in Rome
O n your plate you will mostly get spaghetti
M ost people talk a foreign language in Rome
E nter the French Alps and you might meet a friendly yeti!

Emma Hughes (8)
St Oliver Plunkett's Primary School, Ballyhegan

Frost

When it's frosty and you're outside
You slip and slide
It looks like fun
When it's frosty and you're outside.

When it's frosty and you're outside
It looks like fun
But it can be dangerous
When it's frosty and you're outside.

When it's frosty and you're outside
You have to defrost your car
You may be late for school
When it's frosty and you're outside.

When it's frosty and you're outside
It gleams like silver
Sometimes you can't see it
When it's frosty and you're outside.

When it's frosty and you're outside
It's very cold
You wrap up warm
When it's frosty and you're outside.

Karla Rogers (9)
Windmill Integrated Primary School, Dungannon

When Light Comes From The Sky

When light comes from the sky
You get a fright
Suddenly you're alright
When light comes from the sky
You might get a scare
It feels like a bear is everywhere

When light comes from the sky
You have to hide
Because the bear is alive
When light comes from the sky
You better run because
The light wants to have some fun

When light comes from the sky
You run down the street
Go in your house.

Ryan Graham—McCurry (9) & Luke Ferguson
Windmill Integrated Primary School, Dungannon

Pink And Black

Pink
Happy, fun
Pictures, sleepovers, hearts
Playful, dark, funny, dull
Scaring, shocking, gulping
Terrible, frightening
Black.

Emily Elliott—Murphy (10)
Windmill Integrated Primary School, Dungannon

My Cats

Small and furry
Cute mammals
Milk lover
Lovely and playful
Soft and round
Dog hater
Lazy mammals
Meat eater
People lover
Fun lover
Good jumper
Ball chaser
Self licker
Miaow caller.

Lauryn Donaghy (8)
Windmill Integrated Primary School, Dungannon

The Butterfly

Amazing insect
Beautiful colours
Intelligent insect
Light flier
Wonderful hearing
Big wings
Quiet insect
Very shy
Waterproof skin
Garden lover.

Katie Burns (8)
Windmill Integrated Primary School, Dungannon

When It Snows

When it snows, when it snows,
It makes everything look white,
It falls silently as a mouse.

When it snows, when it snows,
We throw it at each other,
We make people out of it.

When it snows, when it snows,
It makes us feel happy,
It reminds us of winter.

When it snows, when it snows,
It makes everything look white,
It falls silently as a mouse.

Andrew Graham (9)
Windmill Integrated Primary School, Dungannon

Cats

Very fluffy
Cute, cuddly
Walks about
Likes mice and birds
Loves playing
Loves food
Very clever
Lives with people
Sometimes eats meat
I love cats.

Ciara Cairns (8)
Windmill Integrated Primary School, Dungannon

133

Thunder

When it's thundery outside
Your electric goes out
It's quite a shock
When it's thundery outside

When it's thundery outside
You jump with a shock
And it's quite a surprise
When it's thundery outside

When it's thundery outside
It's very scary
So prepare to be shocked
When it's thundery outside.

Benjamin Cunningham (8)
Windmill Integrated Primary School, Dungannon

When The Sun Shines

When the sun shines
It makes the flowers grow.

When the sun shines
It lights up everything

When the sun shines
It makes grass grow
And fruit grow on trees.

When the sun shines
It makes the air
Feel nice and warm.

Nakita Beattie (8)
Windmill Integrated Primary School, Dungannon

Sunshine

Sunshine is very bright
And it makes us warm

When it shines
It warms us up
And makes us tired

Flowers need to be watered
And wasps and bees
Come around

Its colours are bright
And yellow
And it is very nice and calm.

Laura Maye (8)
Windmill Integrated Primary School, Dungannon

When The Sun Comes Out

When the sun comes out,
I come out to play.
When my friends come over,
We go and play.

But when the sun goes away,
We go inside and play.
So go out and enjoy the sun while you can,
But when it goes down you can't go out.

When I come inside,
When the sun goes down,
I watch TV and go to bed.

Naomi Symington (9)
Windmill Integrated Primary School, Dungannon

My Kitten

Small, furry
Cute, clever
Scatty, strong
Mammal, wild
Playful, shiny
Dog hater
Soft, special
Lovely, shy
Kitten, purr
Likes fish
Sleeps lots
A lovely friend.

Caitlin Lynch (8)
Windmill Integrated Primary School, Dungannon

The Sea

The sea can be furious
The sea can be mad
The sea can be crazy
The sea can be bad
The sea can smash
The sea can roar like a hungry bear.
The sea can be peaceful
The sea can be quiet
The sea can be still.
The sea can be calm as a sleeping cat.
The sea can creep over the sand,
Stroking the beach like a giant hand.

Adam McClean (9)
Windmill Integrated Primary School, Dungannon

Volcano William

I switched on the TV.
Football!
Where was 'You've Been Framed'?
My voice blasted and rumbled.
I roared, 'I hate football!'
Then I erupted, 'It isn't coming on!'
I exploded.
I was bursting, frothing and furious.
I cried because I was sad that I had been angry.
I was like a volcano recovering from its eruption.
Quietly rumbling.

William Lanigan (9)
Windmill Integrated Primary School, Dungannon

Snow Leopards

Very vicious
Fast predator
Big mammal
Lots of energy
Breathes air
Gives birth
Very strong
Protects its cubs
Hunts prey
Marvellous mammal.

Corey McGurgan (8)
Windmill Integrated Primary School, Dungannon

Tigers

Big predator
Lethal stalker
Big and furry
Sharp teeth
Feeds cubs
Black stripes
Sharp claws
Big paws
Bad behaviour
Lives in India.

Tyler Kennedy (7)
Windmill Integrated Primary School, Dungannon

Goldfish

Small slippery
Different colours
Loves water
Bubble blower
Three second memory
Gobbles food
Hates cats
Shiny scales
Colourful fins
Lovely creatures.

Rachel Nicholson (8)
Windmill Integrated Primary School, Dungannon

My Brother

Cute, cuddly
Small, funny
Annoying boy
Lovely boy
Playful person
Loves cars
Kind fellow
Likes tickles
Laughs lots
Nice kid.

Shannon McCaul (7)
Windmill Integrated Primary School, Dungannon

My Poem

When it is sleeting
I go under my sheet
And tickle my feet
And eat Shredded Wheat
And look out the window
In the icy cold night
Then in the morning it is really bright
Then I go out in the bad sleet weather
Everyone is freezing and the teacher is too.

Cameron Donaghy (9)
Windmill Integrated Primary School, Dungannon

Happiness

H appy world and feel joyful
A ll laugh loud
P layful and loves a hug
P ity when it goes away
I nside feels warm
N obody hates happiness
E nergetic in a happy world
S ometimes wants to jump around
S miling makes you glow.

Jake Bell (8)

Windmill Integrated Primary School, Dungannon

Happiness

H appiness is a good feeling
A ll happiness is great
P eople feel great when you play
P eople like to be happy
I have a great feeling
N ice and joyful
E nergy is a good feeling
S miling is very cheerful
S miling is infectious.

Shannon Fox (8)

Windmill Integrated Primary School, Dungannon

Angriness

A horrible feeling
N othing good
G ross inside
R ubbish
I n a bad world of your own
N othing is good
E mptiness inside
S ucks
S uper when it goes away.

Jodie Boyd (8)
Windmill Integrated Primary School, Dungannon

Rugby

Boys' game
Really tough
Oval ball
Dirty muck
Always cold
Always good
Running fast
Scoring tries.

Jack Kennedy (8)
Windmill Integrated Primary School, Dungannon

Butterfly

Wonderful creature
Very pretty
Garden lover
Interesting insect
Great colours
Very quiet
Bright wings
Waterproof skin.

Emily Lanigan (7)
Windmill Integrated Primary School, Dungannon

When It Snows

When it snows
It is cold on your nose
When it snows

When it snows
You go out to play
It is cold on your toes
When it snows.

Paige Cassidy (9)
Windmill Integrated Primary School, Dungannon

Fire And Water

Fire
Hot, red
Burning, scorching, blazing
Burning and melting, splashing and alive
Rocks, splashes, sways
Cold, blue
Water.

Tyler Clarke (10)
Windmill Integrated Primary School, Dungannon

Sadness

S adness is a very hurtful feeling
A very unhappy feeling
D ark feeling
N ever anyone to talk to
E ach day a misery
S ucks
S uper when it goes away.

Aoife Haggan (7)
Windmill Integrated Primary School, Dungannon

Exciting And Boring

Exciting
Joyful, cheerful
Football, tennis, golf
Activities, washing, parties, work
Sleeping, waiting, silence
School, chores
Boring.

Jacob Cunningham (9)

Windmill Integrated Primary School, Dungannon

Elephant And Mouse

Elephant
Big, strong
Stomping, drinking, walking
Big floppy ears, squeaky little animal
Squeaking, eating, sleeping
Small, thin
Mouse.

Cameron Sloss (9)

Windmill Integrated Primary School, Dungannon

Loving

L oving might make you happy
O h I love my family
V ery nice
I love the sound of music
N ice morning to have
G ood friend.

Teah Cullen (8)
Windmill Integrated Primary School, Dungannon

Sunshine

The sunshine makes me feel happy.
Its colour is sunny.
The sound makes everyone feel happy.
It reminds me of summer.

Kasia Kozuch (9)
Windmill Integrated Primary School, Dungannon

Young Writers Information

We hope you have enjoyed reading this book - and that you will continue to enjoy it in the coming years.

If you like reading and writing poetry drop us a line, or give us a call, and we'll send you a free information pack.

Alternatively if you would like to order further copies of this book or any of our other titles, then please give us a call or log onto our website at www.youngwriters.co.uk

Young Writers Information
Remus House
Coltsfoot Drive
Peterborough
PE2 9JX
(01733) 890066